CW01095381

An Inspirational Treasury

mabel c jones

WESTBOW
PRESS®
A DIVISION OF THOMAS NELSON
& ZONDERVAN

Copyright © 2020 mabel c jones.

All rights reserved. No part of this book may be used or reproduced by
any means, graphic, electronic, or mechanical, including photocopying,
recording, taping or by any information storage retrieval system
without the written permission of the author except in the case of
brief quotations embodied in critical articles and reviews.

WestBow Press books may be ordered through booksellers or by contacting:

WestBow Press
A Division of Thomas Nelson & Zondervan
1663 Liberty Drive
Bloomington, IN 47403
www.westbowpress.com
1 (866) 928-1240

Because of the dynamic nature of the Internet, any web addresses or
links contained in this book may have changed since publication and
may no longer be valid. The views expressed in this work are solely those
of the author and do not necessarily reflect the views of the publisher,
and the publisher hereby disclaims any responsibility for them.

Any people depicted in stock imagery provided by Getty Images are
models, and such images are being used for illustrative purposes only.
Certain stock imagery © Getty Images.

Scripture taken from the King James Version of the Bible.

ISBN: 978-1-9736-9495-3 (sc)
ISBN: 978-1-9736-9497-7 (hc)
ISBN: 978-1-9736-9496-0 (e)

Library of Congress Control Number: 2020911812

Print information available on the last page.

WestBow Press rev. date: 11/11/2020

Contents

Foreword

What a blessing and an honor to be a part of a project of powerful meditation and inspiring poetry! Inside you will find some remarkable, delightful, thought-provoking, and heart-grabbing words of wisdom and life testimonies as this author inspires, uplifts, and comforts you with the art of poetry. She has a story to tell through poetry that will speak life into those dry bones. Poetry in motion is what I call it. Each poem will take you through a journey to help you realize yes, those tiny details in our busy lives matter! Her poetry is like a prescription for your mind, heart, soul, and body. You will be encouraged to know that even when your life is broken, her writing will help you pick up the right pieces to put your life back together again. We all have a story, and it's a powerful one, even when it's a mess. She is fearfully and wonderfully made, and her writing exhibits that in every sense of the word.

An Inspirational Treasury is sure to bring life to your hopelessness and joy to your sorrows as you recover from any brokenness or are just walking through life. This collection of reflections should become a part of your library. In this book, you will find words that will touch and uplift your heart. And I don't just say that because she is my mother; it is genuinely true! I hope you'll enjoy reading it as much as I have. It's a treasured blessing!

Lori Stokes, AA, BA, MBA

Preface

Thank you for this opportunity to be an encouragement to you. For that is why I wrote these poems. Each one is inspired by a moment in my life when things were good or bad, or I was just thinking of something to use to encourage someone. Or maybe I was in the store, in the park, or sitting on the riverbank. Or perhaps I was talking to my children or a friend, listening to a sermon or a song, or even asleep, and the words just came into my mind. Sometimes they were all at once, and I wrote the whole poem in minutes. Sometimes it was just a word or a sentence, and weeks or even months later, I finished the rest of the poem. But I always knew it would be an encouragement to someone at some time.

My family and friends kept telling me I ought to write a book. I kept telling me, "One day." But the writing was in me, and it just kept coming. I put it off almost all my life and followed other endeavors. And even for a while, I did not write at all. Finally, I returned to my writing, and I knew this was where my calling was. So I take this opportunity to share with you this first book. I have already started two more, one a short story and one another book of poems. But both just to encourage someone, everyone, who reads them that God will see them through whatever storm life takes them into because He is the Way to your answer, whatever right answer you're looking for. My testimony is I am saved, sanctified, and Holy Ghost–filled. I have attended church all my life. I have been a member of a Baptist church, a COGIC church, and now a PAW church because that's the way God has led me. I love the Lord with all my heart. He has never failed me yet, and I don't look for any failure in Him ever, only the victory He's always given me. Oh, I've had good seasons and bad seasons, but in it all and through it all, I've learned the good always outweighs the bad, and that trusting in God always gives me everything I need to make this journey glorious! Praying the very best for you because God's got everything you'll ever need. Thank you.

Acknowledgment

First of all, to God be the glory for this wonderful gift He has given me. To my family—especially my husband, my mother, my children, and my sisters—who have always stood by me and encouraged me from day one in anything I endeavored to do. To my special friends at AAA and LHS, who always told me I should write a book. To my church family and my pastor, Dr. Sylvera T. Greene, who always complimented my writing and encouraged me to write a book. And a special acknowledgment to every person who reads these poems. May God richly bless the moments of your days spent reading these words…a grateful thank you!

Dedicated to and in loving memory of my lifelong sweetheart and husband of 48+ years: Andrew Jones

Introduction

A book of prose and poetry to encourage and inspire you along your walk with God, that no matter what the situation, circumstance, trial, test, or tribulation to never lose heart or give up because God's got this ... *always*.

By Faith

Believe what you pray,

Not what you see.

And by faith

God will cause it to be—

Maybe not today or tomorrow,

But with His Word, let it agree.

Keep on believing;

He will cause it to be.

LIFE Matters!

Some say Black lives matter

And they do

But where does that leave

Brown and Yellow

And Red and White—

And Interracial lives?

Some say all lives matter

And they do

But more truly…

Life matters—because

That covers all races,

Genders and ages—

And includes

All socio-economic groups, too

Life matters—because

Out of the dust of the earth

God made us in His own image

He gave us life and said, 'Go,

Be fruitful and multiply,
And have dominion upon the earth'
He didn't say anything
About color or race
He just made us all
And breathed this Life into us all
No matter what the color or race
Then many years later,
He sent a Saviour, Jesus Christ
His precious blood to shed—
Who gave His Life
For one…for all
No matter what the color or race
And that is the true story
Of why Life matters today
And always will surpass
What any color or race barrier
Tries to make matter
One other thing, though…
This Jesus arose on the third day—
And once again…Life matters!
And triumphs over
Color and race,
Gender and age,

And socio-economic status

So, when you march

With your banner,

Or proudly wear your t-shirt

Remember—

It's not about any color or race

But it is that Life matters

Because,

When you think about it—

Aren't we all of some color…

Anyway?!

Word Weapon

There is no life storm too boisterous

That God can't calm with a "Peace; be still."

That's His word weapon.

By the way…

You are welcome to use it too!

Numbered, Not Counted

The hairs of your head
Are numbered by God.
You can't even count them;
You can only color them, temporarily.
But He knows them by number,
And He knows every numbered location,
Length, width at base and tip, and age.
He knows the one that came out in your brush,
And the one that came out in your comb,
And exactly where it came from on your head.
And He knows what you are thinking
When you are secretly combing, brushing, smoothing
Trying to cover that bald spot—
He knows and He's got them numbered.
Now, Friend, that's some kind of caring!

The Rough Side

If it were up to us,

There would be no

Rough side of the mountain.

Just a smooth, easy slope,

But the rough side

Is the side with something

To grip and hold onto.

Something to allow us to daily

Move on up a little higher.

It's the side where God and His Word

Will guide you every step of the way.

Keep gripping …

And climbing …

And praising.

And never let go or give up

Because that rough side

Is the side of your *victory!*

New Day Today

Of course it's a new day every day,

Because God's mercies

Are new every day.

And we dare not miss

An opportunity any day

To give Him total praise,

To serve Him with our whole heart,

And to win others along the way.

Ahh, thank You for another new day!

PLUS!

P—Peace

L—Love

U—Unity

S—Strength

Claim the PLUS of Jesus

For your life today and every day.

It's available... *just for your asking!*

Just So You Know

There is no sadder thing in this life

Than to live and to die and to go to hell

When all you needed for your salvation

Was to accept Jesus Christ as your Saviour

And ask Him to forgive your sin.

Salvation and heaven just for the asking—

I encourage you to choose Jesus today!

Because today may be your last opportunity.

You'll be shouting glad you did—

For the rest of your life.

And that, just so you know,

Will be for eternity!

I Shall Not Be Moved.

I shall not be moved.

How important is that *shall* to you?

Is it important enough for you

To attend church every Sunday,

Not just out of habit or for social reasons

But because you really, really love the Lord?

Is it important enough for you

To stay from opening greeting

To closing benediction?

To give your worship undivided attention?

To the point of muting your cell phone

To get involved in the praise?

To the point of raising your voice and hands?

How important is that *shall* to you?

Is it important enough for you

To be there, rain or shine,

Cold or hot, snow or not?

To choose Wednesday prayer meeting

Or Wednesday Bible study

Instead of Wednesday card party

Or Wednesday movie night

Or a midweek night out with friends?

Just how important is that *shall* to you?

Is it important enough to you

To lay aside every weight or distraction

That so easily besets or entangles you

And choose to be in a church service

Rather than anywhere else?

Just how important is that *shall* to you?

Is it important enough to do

Whatever it takes down here on earth

To make your choice heaven instead of hell?

"I shall not be moved."

Are you just singing words of a song,

Or are you singing a promise to God?

Just how important is that *shall* to you?

Thankful

I'm thankful for the joy and faith
That fill my heart each day
And give me hope and strength
To make this journey all the way.

I'm thankful for the power of healing
Vested in those thirty-nine stripes revealing.
I'm thankful for the cross on Calvary,
Where You shed Your precious blood for me.

I'm thankful for that lowly stable room
And for the victory of that empty tomb.
I'm thankful for Your precious, holy Word;
It keeps me focused and assured.

I'm thankful for Your mercy and Your grace
That provide me courage to run this race.
I'm thankful for Your endless love
And for the promise of heaven above.

And I'm so very thankful for salvation

For it is a holy invitation

To live for all eternity

With Jesus, who gave His all for me.

O Lord,

From the bottom of my heart,

Without any further ado,

I am just so very, very thankful for You!

The S-S-S Factor

Saved, sanctified, satisfied.
Saved by Jesus's precious blood,
Sanctified and Holy Ghost filled,
And so satisfied that I won't ever look back—
That's His S-S-S factor working in me.

Soothed, sweetened, steered.
He soothes all my hurts,
He sweetens all my bitterness,
And He steers me into righteous paths along the way.
And again, His S-S-S factor is working in me.

Seeking, studying, strengthening.
Seeking more of Jesus each and every day,
Studying His Word to show myself approved,
And strengthening any weakness with
His mustard-seed faith.
And again, His S-S-S factor is at work in me.

And when I can't find my way, can't see my way,

Don't even know what my next step will be,

I have only to look to Jesus.

He is the Way, is always, in all ways, the Way.

And there it is again; His S-S-S factor is at work in me.

Ahh, that's soul-saving satisfaction!

In Spite of It All—Hope

There is a hope that can supersede all despair.

There is a hope that can transcend all discouragement.

There is a hope that can reverse any doubt.

There is a hope that is beyond all hope.

And that hope is birthed by your faith.

And faith is founded in God and His Word.

Surely God will make a way out of no way

Because He *is* the Way.

He said He'd never forsake us or leave us alone,

Therefore, hope—

In spite of anything, in spite of everything,

No matter what you're going through,

Hope on—

Even when it seems there is nothing left,

There is always that bit of inexhaustible hope within

Trust God, and hold on to your hope.

In spite of it all—hope.

Choose Ye This Day

There is a blood-stained cross
And streets where needless blood was shed—
Choose ye this day.

There is a way straight from His Word
And a highway crooked and deceiving—
Choose ye this day.

There is a place of joy unspeakable
And a place of sorrow and gnashing of teeth—
Choose ye this day.

There is a race not given to the swift
But one that can be won by endurance and faith—
Choose ye this day.

There is One who gave His all just for you;
I offer you Jesus—
Choose ye this day.

Don't Be Afraid; Be Prepared

You walk through this life day-by-day,
Ever searching for just the right path
To lead you and guide you along your way.

While searching you see in your sight there is
More than one way, more than one path to trod.
Don't let fear creep in; make your choice; be prepared.

Know that no matter what it may be,
God is always by your side if you seek guidance,
And He will always give you a sure victory.

And when your time winds into twilight years,
There's no need to wonder or be afraid
If with Jesus you've made your choice and prepared.

For it's the choice you make in your time here
That makes your eternal choice joy-filled.
And alas, having chosen Jesus, you have prepared!

No Ending;
Only Eternity

Runnin', runnin',

Believe I'll jus' run on.

See what the end's gonna be.

Then I heard a voice say,

"No ending here, only eternal joy ahead!"

Then I raised my hands and answered with a shout,

"Amen, Lord!"

No trial or test could stop me now!

Sickness only slowed me for a moment,

But I kept on runnin', runnin'

Faster, more determined now.

Runnin' and not weary.

Believe I'll jus' run on, Lord, I shouted again!

See what eternity's gonna be!

He smiled and said,

"Come on, my Child, I've blocked every obstacle.

Your path is clear and I won't let you fail."

Listenin' to His voice

Runnin' with me and hailin' me on

I heard the praises of the many before me

Nothin' could stop me now—

Then we crossed over together

And eternity was all that He'd promised

With no end in sight

Awesome God!

Awesome eternity!

Glory hallelujah!!

Nothing Wrong
with Right

You can search the world over,
And everywhere you look,
You will find there is wrong
And there is right,
And there is nothing wrong with right.

You may find those who protest
That there is something wrong with right
Because they have chosen wrong to seek.
But right stands true all by itself
For there is nothing wrong with right.

If you choose wrong,
The pitfalls take you there.
If you choose right,
The experiences take you there.
For there is nothing wrong with right.

There is One whose name is Jesus;

He is right all by Himself.

And He won't lead you wrong

If your choice is Him,

You will surely find

There is absolutely nothing—

Nothing wrong with Him being your right!

So You Went to Church Today

Going to church is a good start,

But—

Accepting Jesus Christ

Is the real reason

For what it's all about.

Because you can go to church

All of your life

And still end up in hell.

But—

When you accept Jesus Christ,

He changes your heart and your life.

And now you've made the choice

That will take you all the way to heaven.

A real reason … a real choice … ahh …

Church was good today!

God Always Answers

God always answers.
It may not be the answer you want,
But God always answers.
He'll never, ever leave you
Without an answer.
And whether it is the answer
You are looking for or not,
It is always, *always*,
The right answer for you.
And always right on time.
It may not fit your schedule,
Routine, or plans,
But His answer is according to His plan.
And if you accept it,
You are guaranteed not to fail.
Just pray, trust, believe, wait—
And keep on prayerfully
And faithfully seeking Him.

No matter what the situation,

Circumstance, or timeframe,

God *always* answers.

He always has a plan fit just for you.

Always keep the faith.

Always hold on to His promise.

No matter how long it takes,

Always *know* that God *will* answer

Because God is the answer—

Waiting to be your answer.

He's waiting on you

To grow to your season of a blessed answer.

God never fails; He's always on time,

And yes, it's Word-guaranteed—

That He will answer...always!

Can God?

Can He save lost souls?
You know He can;
He saved you

Can He turn darkness into light?
You know He can;
He is the Light

Can He heal every sickness?
You know He can;
He healed you

Can He fix any problem, big or small?
You know He can,
Because there is no failure in Him

Is there is anything that's impossible for God?
You know there isn't;
He's the I AM in impossible

So don't ever be discouraged by what you see, feel, or hear.

You know what His Word says: just ask and believe—

Even when a wait is involved

Because God can—

Oh, yes, He can—

By faith, you know He can!

Proof Positive

It's not just another fairy tale that has been passed down
Without a confirmation to be found.

It's not just another rumor that someone has spread
To try and outdo what someone else has said.

But it's an absolute, genuine, historical, Bible-grounded truth
That Jesus Christ was born; an empty tomb is living proof!

More than Just
Another Book

So you think it's just another book,

Not worthy of your time or attention.

Two covers enclosing just another book,

Not to be compared to your life's intention.

But the Holy Bible is more than just another book

To gather dust there on your shelf or mantle,

With other prized possessions to be seen but not touched,

On display like a sensuous aromatic candle.

For it is the Word of God in all its glory,

And full of splendor in its every jot and tittle

That will touch and stir and draw your heart,

And transform your whole being more than just a little.

It is those sixty-six books within that Book

That repeat the words of Jesus Christ and tell His story

Of how He suffered and shed His precious blood
To redeem us one and all; to Him be all the glory!

The Holy Bible is more than just another book.
Its story can't be proven unfounded, ungrounded, or untrue.
Its whole story cannot be told in any one book
Because in its Author's omniscience its truth is rooted too.

No, not just another book whose words go on and on.
Nor just another book to hold a space upon your shelf.
But a Book of Love and Peace and Joy and Hope.
A book that transforms our minds and hearts to Jesus code.

God's Holy Word, so much more than just another book.
It is a lifeline to our souls prepared with love
To redeem us from a world of sin and shame,
And lead us to a life eternal prepared in heaven above.

One Thing
I Know

One thing I know,

One thing I will always live by,

Jesus is all the world to me,

And Jesus will see me through it all.

Well, that's two things, you say.

No, it's One—JESUS!

There Is None, None like Him

There is none, none like Him.
You can search the world over,
And no matter where you look—
Be it north, south, east, or west,
No matter what city, town, state,
Country or continent—
Be it high or low, here or there,
You will find there is none,
Nowhere that can compare to Him.
You might think you've found a match,
But, step back; don't let yourself be deceived,
Take a closer look and you'll see,
Oh, no, there *is* absolutely none,
None like Jesus!

Ever Moving,
Never Hiding

God is ever moving.

He never hides;

If you can't find Him,

Look in His Word.

Say a prayer.

Sing a praise.

Ahh, now you feel Him—

There He is,

Moving—moving in you.

Now Is the Time

Don't put off till tomorrow
What was yesterday's opportunity
To choose righteousness—
And now could become today's
Wish-I-would-have-listened-and-obeyed.
Now is the time of salvation—
Tomorrow may very well be too late.

A Believer

Everybody's a Jesus Christ

believer in hell—

but then,

it'll be too late;

Now is your only

door of opportunity,

to believe and to choose

To make your choice

Before it's too late

To choose to believe the truth of Jesus and His Word

Instead of the lies and deception of the devil

To choose to be a Believer

Absolutely, positively, and eternally!

All I Wanted for Christmas

You may not have gotten what or all

You wanted for Christmas—

But you can get all you need

And many of your desires

By trusting and delighting yourself

Anytime, any season—

By faith in Jesus and His Word!

Absolutely That Important

Is it really that important?
Yes, it is absolutely that important!
And oh, it is only found in Jesus,
Who shed His blood to make it absolutely so
For He is our only hope, our only answer.
Claim Him by faith; trust and believe,
And you'll find Him to be
Most definitely—
Absolutely that important!

Ride with Me

Ride with Me
A little while,
And I will give you rest.
Ride with Me
A little while longer,
And your victory's in sight.
Ride with Me,
And I will show you the way
I AM the Way.
Ride with me
Hold on,
No matter what; don't let go.
Ride with Me
And always remember—
I will never forsake you.
Ride with Me
For this one reason:
I AM the Way.

He's a Keeper

Ain't nothin' like the real thing,

But the real thing …

Jesus!

Try Him; you'll see

He's a Keeper!

No Greater Love

For God so loved …

That He suffered unimaginable

Pain, suffering, torture, humiliation.

Then they stretched out His arms

And nailed Him to a cross.

But those nails weren't necessary to hold Him

For God so loved

Us, you and me.

It was His love that held Him on that cross.

His precious blood He shed.

He was crucified and died.

They buried Him in a borrowed tomb,

Borrowed because He wouldn't need it long.

Then He arose on the third day.

No greater love

Because He, Himself, is Love!

And it's His love today

That is still reaching out

To us … to you … to me,

Saying, "No need to search any further.

No need to search anywhere else.

What you're looking for, I AM.

Come, follow me.

My love knows no end,

No condition, no boundary,

No time limit.

My love is fo' real, real,

And it's Word-guaranteed

For I AM love."

No Greater Love!

Because You Chose to Follow Jesus

Because you chose to follow Jesus,

Tests and trials just came out of nowhere.

Because you chose to follow Jesus,

The devil made bad things happen unexpectantly.

Because you chose to follow Jesus,

Friends and even family turned their backs on you.

Because you chose to follow Jesus.

But because you chose to follow Jesus,

Jesus chose to see you through it all.

And now because you chose to follow Jesus,

Through His grace and mercy

And by your faith in His Word,

You got a praise.

You got a shout.

You got the victory.

You got what nobody

And nothing can take away.

Just because you chose to follow Jesus!

Love ... Always

My Child:

To everything there is a time—

To everything there is a season—

Except to love...

Its time—

Its season—

Is always ...

Because God is love,

And God is—

Abundantly always—

Love ... always,

Me (God).

Be Ye Faithful

Our God is faithful.

You remain faithful.

Suddenly,

At His set time,

He will perform

His promise to you.

It is on schedule,

In transit.

To be delivered

As promised

To you.

Our God is faithful.

You remain faithful,

Believing His every word

Shall surely come to pass

Just like He said.

And no amount of time

Will change or deter it

Because if He said it,

Suddenly,

At His set time,

It will come to pass.

Our God is faithful,

And His Word is absolutely sure.

You remain faithful,

And you will see it come to pass

Just like He promised it will.

Our God is faithful.

Be ye also faithful!

Empty Cross, Empty Grave

It had been just three grievous days ago
That my Lord had bled and suffered so.
For they'd beaten and tortured Him, you know,
And esteemed Him lower than low.

His love for humankind is measured by
Those thirty-nine stripes He took without a sigh,
An empty, blood-stained cross where He chose to die,
And an empty grave where His burial
clothes were found to lie.

How His mother must have sorrowed on that day,
To see her firstborn go that way.
At His cross she chose to stand and stay.
In her heart she wished she could take it all away.

He took the opportunity to save a thief there.
On each side of Him they hung, for they were a pair.
One scorned Him and even now didn't care.
The other chose Jesus, His heavenly home to share.

Even in dying, the women stayed there by His side.
Heartbroken, grieved, and torn they cried.
They were last at the grave when He died.
First at the grave that morn they arrived.

The empty grave still serves as witness today
For a mighty great stone was rolled away.
And our Lord and Saviour arose that day,
Triumphant over the price He had had to pay!

Now that empty cross, that empty grave
Where He once hung, where He once laid
Is proof enough to me that Jesus still saves
And that His Word is truth and never fades.

Reach and Believe

Got a vision?

Got a dream?

Reach for it!

Even if your reach misses,

You've stretched your faith,

And that's worth the reach.

Now keep on reaching,

Believing, and trusting God.

And inch by inch,

You'll find your reach

Growing closer and closer

Till one day you'll reach

And grab that vision or dream!

Be sure to give a shout out—

Thank You, Jesus!

Amen and hallelujah!

For your belief has overcome—

Your reach has conquered,

And Jesus has blessed you with your victory!

Choose Ye This Day

There is a blood-stained cross
And the dangerous streets
Where needless blood is shed
Choose ye this day

There is a Way
Straight from His Word
And a highway crooked and deceiving
Choose ye this day

There is a place of eternal joy unspeakable
And a place of eternal sorrow
And gnashing of teeth
Choose ye this day

There is a race that will be won
By love, faith, and trusting God
And there is a race that will be lost without it
Choose ye this day

There is One Who shed His blood for you
There is one who cares not at all
And only desires to see you in hell with him
Choose ye this day

There is One Who gave His all just for you
Because He loves you so;
I offer you JESUS—
Choose ye this day

The Blank Page

So inviting …
Yet so challenging—
What can I do with it?
I cannot leave it blank—
I must write something;
I must put some words on it
Words of encouragement …
Edification, and strength,
So others can read
And be renewed,
Revived, and restored.
There is a therapy in words
That can give the healing
And hope they bespeak.
But also can give the misery
And torment they bespeak.
So as I stare at this blank page,
I wonder what to write.

And then it came to me.

I know just what I'll say

That will stir each reader

To courage and renewing:

Yes, and Amen!

Never doubt, never stress.

Never worry, just be assured.

Jesus says

Nothing is impossible with God.

Pray His Word and believe it

For it leaves no blank page.

Only a Yes and Amen!

That's a Wrap!

Christ in me.

Me in Christ.

His blood He shed

To set me free.

That's a wrap!

That cannot be denied,

Defiled, or defeated.

A wrap that will supply

All my needs

According to His riches in glory

And all the desires of my heart.

Because my desires are

Wrapped up in Him.

Christ in me.

Me in Christ.

I abide in Him.

He abides in me.

That is a wrap!

So that no matter where I go
Or wherever I may be,
Jesus in me, we are a wrap!
And that more than wraps up enough
To make me more than a conqueror
And an overcomer of any obstacle
Ever first to ever last,
My all yielded to His all.

Christ in me.
Me in Christ.
A wrap-sure.
He is my true hope of glory.
Now that *is* a wrap!

The Empty Chair

It was just another Mothers' Day,

A time to go to church like Momma say.

Squirming in the seat I sat,

Wondering what the preacher meant

For I'd only come by standing invitation

And to quench my mom's aggravation.

Mother, she sat still beside me,

A smile on her face so proudly.

I just hoped for this to be over and done

'Cause I had to make me a street run.

"The doors are open," I finally heard the preacher say.

"Won't you let Christ come in and change your life today?"

Then he stepped down from the pulpit intently

And began walking up my aisle purposely.

With arms outstretched, his invitation came.

"Come to Jesus. You will never be the same."

Someone placed a chair up front.

Who would dare to do such a stunt?

I felt a prick upon my heart.

It was so strange, it gave me a start.

What can this be? This empty chair,

Is it for me? Just sitting there …

I looked around to see

If anyone was watching me.

Why was my seat so uncomfortable just now?

Oh, no, was the preacher coming toward me? Oh, wow!

Again, my glance came upon that empty chair.

It was as if it was staring at me … just sitting there.

I looked around. Could I just get out of here?

Eyes seeming to look at me while singing praises joyfully.

Then the preacher stopped and looked my way.

He smiled, and through the singing I heard him say,

"Jesus loves you, don't you know?

For the Bible tells me so.

He's reaching out to you today.

He wants to wash all your sin away.

Right now, all you who are bound can be set free.

If you choose Jesus, the devil will have to flee.

Right now, if you'll touch Him,

He'll touch you back again,

And your life will begin anew,

Just like He promised you!"

My eyes couldn't stop staring at that empty chair.

Why was it empty and just sitting there?
Now I just kept feeling this tug within my heart,
As though it was breaking apart.
Oh, what was this happening to me?
Well I'm just going to get up and leave.
As I stood up, I could no longer ignore the tug bout.
I felt my steps taking me forward instead of out.
I could no longer feel the shackles of my street prison
That had bound me for so long in indecision.
I had forgotten about everybody and everything.
Above me I could actually hear angels sing.
Behind me was unimportant noise.
Beside me I felt my mother's praise and joy.
Before me I felt the love of Jesus there,
Just drawing me to that empty chair.
Step by step I walked forward anxiously.
The preacher reached out for my hand and hugged me.
Now I felt the tears flowing down my cheek,
But I felt strong, no longer lost and weak.
I felt myself sit down, the chair no longer empty.
But it could never contain the joy bubbling within me.
"Hallelujah!" I heard someone shout.
Then I realized it was me, without a doubt.
Yes, my life has changed to brand new.
Now I boldly offer Jesus and the empty chair to you!

That One Colt, That One Destiny

It must have been

Just another day in this man's life.

As he went into his barn

To begin his chores that day,

For he knew his one and only horse

Was about to give birth

To a foal sired by a neighbor's donkey.

As he went about doing his chores,

He kept a watchful eye on his mare.

The day wore on and into late evening,

He began to take notice that his horse was in foal.

As she went to her knees and then lay completely down,

He heard her moaning turn into groaning.

He knew it was now her time to give birth.

Straightway he put all his chores aside

And went to kneel by his mare's side.

He petted her and talked kindly to her,

And with anticipation and caring,

He kept watch over her.

Others came into the barn to offer assist to him,

But he proudly let them know

This was his only mare,

And he would see her through to delivery.

As they all stood back to watch,

Slowly it began.

First he could see the hooves,

And then the legs beginning to poke out.

Then he saw the head,

And within a short eight minutes,

The colt was born!

Then the man watched as the colt struggled to stand

And finally stood stumbling, and then stood straight.

He could feel a special assignment on this colt.

The mare stood and nuzzled her colt

Till he came to her and gave suck.

Then the hours turned into days,

The days turned into weeks,

The weeks turned into months,

And the man watched that mare and colt

As they bonded and the colt grew.

He became a fine specimen of mule flesh

At fourteen hands high and two years old.

The man never allowed him to be ridden

For he felt this colt to be destined

For something bigger than an ordinary beast of burden.

And he began to prepare this colt

For a destiny the man knew not.

Daily he began to tie a harness rope around him

And to just lead him around the pasture.

Then one day an idea came

To take the colt into town.

He put the rope around him as usual

And began to lead him to a place

That, for now, to the man was unknown.

And sadly but proudly, he tied him to a post.

And then, wiping a tear, he turned and walked away.

Somehow, within himself, the man knew ... the colt knew

That it was the colt's destiny time.

Minutes later, that very day,

Two of Jesus's disciples

Came and took the colt away.

For this his destiny was,

To carry our precious Lord and Savior,

Jesus Christ,

Into Jerusalem that last time before Calvary.

That time so long ago.

This was that one colt, that one destiny.

Is your destiny any less important?

If Jesus had a predestinated appointment for a mule,

Won't you accept He has one for you?

Won't you take this opportunity to seek Him...

And find that God-birthed destiny within yourself?

What You're Looking for Is Not Here

What you're looking for is not where you're looking.

It's like looking in the refrigerator for your shoes

When they are in the bedroom, under your bed,

And were never in the refrigerator at first.

So it is in looking in the street,

Or in partying, or in drugs, or in alcohol,

Or in another person,

For your happiness or pleasure.

Because it is not in the street,

It's not in partying, or in drugs, or in alcohol,

Or even in another person.

Who, by the way, is seeking the same, too,

Regardless of gender.

And you'll never find it anywhere you look.

That's why you keep looking and not finding,

Looking and not seeing,

Looking and not satisfied,

Looking and frustrated,

Looking and just pretending to find—

Or temporarily filling with

Drugs, alcohol, sex, or worse—

And still looking and looking some more

Until you hear, heed, seek, and find it, where it truly is,

There's always going to be a void within you.

Friend, what you keep looking for everywhere,

It can *only* be found in Jesus and His Word!

Ahhh, now you're looking where you need to look!

Uniquely Yours

Every word of God is uniquely yours.

Every word of God has its unique meaning for you.

Its meaning speaks anew to each individual.

Yet at the same time,

It speaks to a whole congregation too—

Live or recorded, right now, today, or tomorrow.

Because there is a uniqueness in God's words

That allows them to speak to one

And to many simultaneously

And yet still have a unique meaning

That is uniquely yours

For any situation or circumstance at any time.

That's the uniqueness of God and His word.

While the uniqueness of its meaning to you

Is still and always uniquely yours!

They Suffered

They suffered many things
By so many.
So many would get His Word.
So many could be saved
By accepting Jesus Christ,
Who shed His precious blood
For so many.
Eleven apostles who refused to give up,
Who made themselves twelve again
After Christ's ascension,
Who refused to let stoning stop them,
Who didn't allow shackles or beatings
Or prison to change their minds
But sang praises to God
Till prison doors opened of themselves.
Who suffered hangings and crucifixions,
Decapitations and exile,
But were still and yet determined

That they would let nothing stop them.

They suffered many things

By so many.

So many would get His Word

That Jesus saves.

And even yet today, after over two thousand years,

Jesus's blood still cleanses all sin.

Jesus's love still saves.

Jesus is still alive, and His arms are still outstretched

To many ... to all ... to whosoever will.

He suffered so many could be saved.

His apostles suffered carrying His Word everywhere

So many would get the opportunity

To call Jesus Lord and Saviour!

Oh, how they suffered...

We thank You, Lord and Saviour!

Nothing Too Hard for Jesus

Nothing too hard for my Jesus.
No nothing's too hard for Him!
Nothing too hard for my Jesus.
No nothing's too hard for Him!
No matter what happens today,
God has said He'll make a way.
And there is nothing, nothing, nothing,
Nothing, nothing, nothing,
No nothing, nothing, nothing's
Too hard for Him!

Move, Mountain, Move!

Move, mountain, move!

Move, mountain, move!

Get on outta my way—

The Word of God says,

In the name of Jesus,

You got to move—

Move, mountain, move!

Confusion, trouble, doubt,

Problems, sickness, stress

Whatever the mountain—

Move, mountain, move!

Move, mountain, move!

Get on outta my way—

The Word of God says,

In the name of Jesus,

You got to move—

Move, mountain, move!

The Power in His Name

Your success is in your struggle.
Your blessing is in your hands raised to heaven.
Your seasons thrive with your determination
Not to give up or count any setback as a loss.
Your confidence is in your deep
Abiding faith against all odds.
Your assurance is in God's Word,
Spoken or written.
Your victory is in holding on
No matter what the storms of life bring.
The darkness of your trial
Just makes the light of Jesus shine brighter.
Nothing that the devil can throw at you
Or use to bind you; or to hinder you,
Or to deceive you; or even to destroy you
Has any power over you—
Because you have the power,
And it's all in the name of Jesus—
Sealed with an *Amen* and a *Hallelujah*!

The Cross Is Empty

The cross is empty—
Nothing remains
But the bloodstains—
Jesus paid the price
For it was His sacrifice
That cleansed and made us sin-free.
A sure victory for you and me—
Hallelujah! Shout it out!
A resurrected Jesus …
And that bloodstained empty cross …
You can't ever make me doubt—
That that's what Jesus's plan was all about!

A Word to the Wise

There is victory in Jesus!

Well isn't that five words?

You may be wondering.

No, just one word—

Jesus!

You see, the victory is in Jesus!

So all you need is Jesus!

He is One Word,

A Word to the wise!

Lightning Source UK Ltd.
Milton Keynes UK
UKHW012027021222
413305UK00006B/36